the GREat Aussie SLaNG booK

by
Eric Spilsted

Illustrated by
Paul Gearside with
Vaughan Campbell

Published by Eric Spilsted Publishing
8 West Street, North Sydney, Australia.
Copyright © Eric Spilsted 1997
ISBN 0 646 32412 8

Printed in Australia by Lion Graphics.

ConTENts

About the author

Born in Sydney, **Eric Spilsted** grew up in the Riverina town of Junee where in shearing sheds and railway yards he had his first contact with real Aussie language.

He spent most of his working life in advertising and currently runs his own publishing business specialising in rugby **football** publications including the weekly publication *Rugby News*.

In many years of **knocking** around lots of good and bad places, he has compiled this **fascinating** collection of Aussie words and phrases which form part of the Australian **way of life.**

Gidday!

So youse want to LEARN to

understand

(or even speak) AUSSie.

Well this little

book will get you started.

We've given you a whole

bunch of everyday

Aussie words like

chooks and DUNNY.

There are many thousands of words, phrases and rhyming slang phrases which are quintessentially Australian. Some have come and gone, others remain in use and every day others emerge.

I have listed here just a few of the more popular Aussie words and phrases for those who want to be reminded of our colourful language, for those who would like to colour their speech a little and for those who simply want to understand what is being said to them.

My thanks to the brilliant illustrator Paul Gearside and his partner Vaughan Campbell for the great cartoons and to the wonderfully talented wog sheila MELinda Vassallo who put the words and pictures together.

My thanks also to my many friends who helped me compile this book. These include my old mates Peter Maxwell and Mike Aronsten, Norman (the big boy of song) Erskine, Phil Haldeman, David (Cracker) Hourn, John Gamble, Bruce Armstrong, Paul Rikk, Tina Higginbotham and Karen Skelton.

Eric Spilsted

Australian
colloquial slang

Aussie slang is **rich** in **clever** and **colourful** description which is **unique** in the **world.**

This **sub-language** evolved in the **Australian bush** and moved to the cities through the **Depression,** two **world wars, post-war immigration** and the **yuppie emergence.**

Like Aussie rhyming slang, **colloquial slang** is heard mostly around the **pubs, clubs** and **racecourses** but **we all use** some of these **phrases** in our **conversation** often **without** really being **aware of it.**

Phrases such as **'dry as a dead dingo's donga', 'flat out like a lizard drinking'** and **'up shit creek without a paddle'** create a vivid word picture not achieved with conventional language.

Try a few in your **conversation.** Your friends will be **amazed.**

We have created a series of **typical** Aussie characters who represent the types of people who would be likely to colour their conversation with sprinklings of classic Aussie slang and rhyming slang. You'll hear them all wherever you go throughout Australia.

John - our hero

He's just an average bloke. He's around 35 to 45 years old, average height and weight, average clothing and hair style, probably has a wife and 2.5 kids, has a mortgage, works in an average job and likes a few beers with his mates.

He enjoys a bit of rugby league or AFL and is not over ambitious. Just a nice average bloke who is mostly good but sometimes naughty.

Harry - the punter

Harry is a somewhat smallish man in his 40's or 50's who can be found around the pubs and racecourses of Australia.

He is a sharp dresser who often has the mandatory pair of field glasses slung around his neck. He wears snappy 'pork pie' hat and rather loud suits.

He is very street-wise and knows a lot of people. They are mostly trainers, jockeys, petty criminals and barmaids.

Harry may be married, but one would never know. He has no interests other than horse racing and drinking at his favourite watering hole.

Mick - the truckie

Mick is large, always wears a
navy blue singlet, is liberally
tattooed, has a hairy chest
and mostly wears shorts and
thongs. He is a hard man who
played football and knows
how to handle himself in a bar
or street fight. He is
essentially good natured and
never gets drunk although he
consumes enormous
quantities of dark beer.

Tim - the yuppie

He is 25 - 35 years old, dresses in the latest fashions, has a styled hairdo, works in advertising, merchant banking or foreign exchange, is often talking on a mobile phone and always frequents the trendiest of bars where he drinks chardonnay. He lives in Paddington or Carlton, is single and is preoccupied with his appearance and his next date.

Jack - the bushie

He's tall, thin and has gaunt features. He comes from somewhere up the scrub and has done a bit of everything. He likes a drink and a chat and is very relaxed and easy going. He speaks with a drawl and wears a broad-brimmed hat which is often surrounded by flies.

Sheila - the girl

She's just your average fun-loving
Aussie girl. She is reasonably tall,
wears tight skirts and has big tits. She
doesn't have a special man, she enjoys
a few beers with the blokes and is
regarded by all as a 'good sport.'

GREAT Aussie Words

A...

acre
Rear end, bum.
'The lazy bastard's out there sitting on his acre.'

aleck
A boastful person who thinks he knows a
lot, but really knows bugger all (nothing)
'He's a smart aleck.'

alley
To 'get a good alley' is to
be in a good position for
the action to follow.

angle of the dangle
An erection.

ankle biter
A child.
'Mum went to
town and took
the ankle biters.'

apples
'She's apples' means that everything
is in good order.
From rhyming slang 'apples and spice' = nice.

arse

Rear end, bum. Has multiple uses:
'Get off your arse' or
'get your arse into gear' - get busy.

'Arse over tit' - describes falling over.

'Arse about face' - something that is
back-to-front. Also 'arse up.'

'Arse beats class' - luck is preferable
to most other skills.

'He has more arse than Jessie' - he has
unusual luck or he is 'very arsey.' (Jessie
was a famous Sydney Zoo elephant)

'He got the arse' - he was fired

from his job.

To get 'a piece of arse' - to achieve
sexual success.

'Pain in the arse' - an annoying person.
'He's a pain in the arse.'

'Make an arse of yourself' - to screw
up badly.

B...

ball and chain   Used by blokes
when talking about their wives, never to
them. Also 'handbrake.'

back door   A homosexual.
bandit   Other terms used by heterosexual
males for gays are:
shirt lifters, pillow biters, toe touchers,
vegemite drillers and chutney packers.

back up   To 'back up' is to have a second
(or third) helping at the dinner table.

bag   'To bag' someone means to disparage or
knock them.
'In the bag' means that the result, like
Chinese elections, is certain.
'Bag your head' is a very strong statement
of disagreement or rejection.

balls and all   Enthusiastic involvement.
'I'll be in that balls and all.'

ball tearer   Someone or something with exceptionally good qualities.
'The game was a real ball tearer.'

balls up   When everything goes wrong, it's a 'proper balls up.'

bang   Sexual intercourse.
'Did you get a bang last night?'

bar   To not have a bar of someone is to choose to have nothing to do with them.
'I won't have a bar of him.'

barbie   An Aussie barbecue.

barrack   Vigorous support of one's football team.
'I barrack for Sydney.'

bash   To have a bash (or burl) at something is to make an attempt at the task.
'I'll give it a bash.'

bastard   A very popular Aussie word which is rarely used to suggest illegitimacy and often used among friends as a term of endearment.
'How are you, you old bastard?' (friendly)
'He's not a bad bastard.' (good)
'He's a poor (unfortunate) bastard.'
'He's a bad bastard.'

battler   Someone who struggles for a livelihood.
'He's a real battler.'

beak   A judge or magistrate.

bearded clam   The female genitalia.

beef bayonet   A penis (curious that these two
should come together here)

bible basher   Someone who is devoutly religious.

big note   A 'big noter' is one who tends to
exaggerate his achievements.

bike   To 'get off one's bike' is to become
angry and lose control.

The 'town bike' is a sexually
promiscuous female - everybody gets
a ride.

bickies   Large sums of money.
'The farm is for sale but
they're talking big bickies.'

bingle   A car crash or 'prang.'

blind Freddie   An imaginary character who represents
a high degree of incompetence.
'The answer is so obvious that even
blind Freddie could see it.'

bloke Aussie men are called blokes.
They're mostly good blokes.

bloody The great Aussie adjective. Can be used
to add emphasis to most words and
usually is. 'Bloody good,' 'bloody awful',
'bloody anything.'

bludger Someone who is lazy and does not pull
his weight. Thus the term 'dole bludger.'

blue A fight.
'He bunged on a blue in the pub.'
or 'I'm blueing with him.'

bog To 'go for a bog' is to defecate.

bog in To start eating.
'Let's bog in.'

boiler Usually an 'old boiler' which means a
woman who is past her prime.

bonk A polite word for a fuck.

bonzer Excellent and deserving of admiration.
'He's a bonzer bloke.'

bollocky Someone 'in the bollocky' is in the nude.

bolter A long-priced winner. Usually a horse.

boofhead A very stupid person.

box
A coarse expression for the female genitalia. Curiously it is also the name of the protecter used by cricketers to guard their private parts.

boobs
Euphemism for women's breasts.

booze bus
The police mobile used for random breath testing.

bo peep
To look.
'Have a bo peep at this.'

bracket
The backside.
'He got a kick up the bracket.'

brass monkey
When a man gets very cold he may be heard to say 'It's so cold, it would freeze the balls off a brass monkey.'

brass razoo
To not have a brass razoo is to be very down and out.

brewers droop
A man's inability to achieve an erection after drinking too much beer.

bugger
A great Aussie word with many uses:
bugger it! - annoyance.
bugger me! - surprise.
bugger off! - get lost!
bugger around - waste time.
buggered if I know - ignorance.
bugger (something) up - spoil, ruin.

bullshit artist Someone who flirts with the truth and is given to gross exaggeration. A politician?

bunch of fives Fist. 'If he doesn't shut up I'll give him a bunch of fives.'

bundle To 'drop one's bundle' is to give up - to surrender all responsibility.

bung it on To put on 'side' or affectation.

burn To 'go for a burn' is to go for a fast car ride.

bush A general term for anywhere outside of the cities. 'He's gone bush.'

bushed One can be totally bushed (lost) or just bushed (exhausted)

bush tucker Food from the bush.

bush week 'What do you think it is - bush week?'
An answer given to a stupid question.

BYOG (BYO) Bring your own grog.
A sign seen in restaurants.

cardie   A cardigan.

cark it   To die.
'Old Charlie carked it.'

charlie   A woman.

chip in   To donate to someone else's cause.

chock-a-block   Full. 'The place was chock-a-block' or
'chockers.'
Sometimes 'chock-a-block up 'er'
meaning sexual success.

choof off   To move along.
'I think I'll choof off.'

chooks   Barnyard fowls which are the prize in the
many 'chook raffles' held in pubs
throughout Australia.

chrome dome   A bald headed man.

chop   To 'get in for your chop' is to grab your fair
share of something.
'Not much chop' means something which is
of doubtful value.

choppers   Teeth.

chuck   To vomit.
'I just had a chuck.'
To throw something.
'I chucked a stone at him.'

chunder   To vomit.
Sometimes called the 'technicolour yawn'
or 'calling for Bert.'

clacker   Bum. 'I kicked him up the clacker.'

clam digger   Penis.

clanger   A bad mistake which one 'drops.'
'During his speech, he dropped a real
clanger!'

clink   Prison. 'They threw him in the clink.'

coat hanger   The Sydney Harbour Bridge.

cobber   A friend, or to use the Aussie term,
mate.

cocky   A farmer as in cow cocky, wheat cocky
etc.

come good   A sudden reversal of otherwise poor
form or conditions.
'Things should soon come good.'

come off it!   A comment of cynical disbelief.

conk out   A machine or person which has or is
about to break down.
'My car's conked out!'

cop it   To take your punishment.
Sometimes 'cop it sweet' which means
taking your punishment with
very good grace.

cossie   Swimming costume.

cracker	'Not worth a cracker' means worth very little.
crack hardy	To put on a brave front.
crack it	To achieve sexual success.
crash hot	An outstanding result. Sometimes 'shit hot' which means the same but is a little more colourful.
crawl	To suck up to authority. 'He's a real crawler.'
crook	Unwell. 'Jeeze I'm feeling crook.' To berate or abuse someone. 'I'll go crook at him when I see him.'
crow	An old or ugly woman.
crumpet	A bit of crumpet is either sexual success - 'I got a bit of crumpet' or an attractive woman who may be seen as 'not a bad bit of crumpet.'
crust	A livelihood. 'What do you do for a crust?'

daggy Someone or something which is unfashionable or grubby.

damage the Doulton To use the lavatory.

date The bum.
'A kick up the date.'

dead marine An empty beer bottle.

dead-set Absolutely true.
'He's a dead-set champion.'

dickhead A fool.

dill Same as above.

dinki-di Very real.
'He's a dinki-di Aussie' or
he's 'real dinkum.'

dip out To withdraw from or lose out.
'I dipped out on the job.'

dob in To inform against someone.
'I'll dob you in to the boss.'

dog's disease Influenza. 'I've got the dog's disease.'

dole bludger   Someone on unemployment benefits and who is not really interested in joining the ranks of the employed.

donkey's years   A long time.
'I haven't seen him for donkey's years.'

down under   A term others use to describe Australia.

drum   Reliable information.
'The jockey gave me the drum about his horse.'

duds   A bloke's duds are his trousers.
A woman's duds are something that blokes want to get into.

dumper   A large wave which breaks suddenly.

dunny   A great Aussie word for the lavatory. Usually the free-standing variety in the backyard.

earbasher   Someone who only stops talking to draw breath.

early opener   A pub which opens earlier in the morning than most.

fair go
To give someone a fair chance to do or say what they wish.

family jewels
Testicles or 'orchestras' if you prefer rhyming slang.

fang farrier
Dentist.

filthy
To be very unhappy with someone. 'I was filthy with him.'

flash
Someone or something which is a bit showy or ostentatious. Conversely, something that is 'not too flash' is a bit below par.

flash it
To offer others a quick peek at one's sexual organ.

flat out
Very busy. 'I can't come today, I'm flat out.'

flick
One can give another the flick (leave them) or get the flick (the sack)

flog
To flog something is to sell it - often under dubious circumstances.

fuck

Has many uses apart from the basic:
fuck about - waste time.
fuck me gently! - suprise.
fuck off - get lost! go away!
fuck you - dismissal, contempt.
fuck all - nothing. 'He knows fuck all.'
fucked - exhausted.
fucked if I know - ignorance.

fuckwit

Don't call someone a fuckwit unless you really mean it and you're bigger than him.

freight

Money. 'Did you bring the freight?'

front up

To make an appearance somewhere, particularly before a judge or magistrate. 'I've got to front up to the beak.'

G...

get-it-interya	A pub term for 'drink up.'
galah	An uncomplimentary term for another. An Australian native bird.
geek	To look. 'Have a geek at this.'
goal	To 'kick a goal' is to have a big win at anything.
gob	Mouth. 'Shut your gob.'
goer	'A real goer' describes someone who is a fast and efficient performer.
goodonyer	Aussie for 'good on you.' Americans say 'have a nice day.' Aussies say 'goodonyer.'
good sort	An attractive woman.

go off   To achieve sexual objectives.
Girls who 'go off' are usually more
sought after than those who don't.
For something to be stolen.
'Don't leave that around, it'll go off.'
To putrefy. 'The milk's gone off.'

gone bung   Broken or unworkable.
'The bloody thing's gone bung.'

gong   An award.
'He got a gong for his community
service.'
Worn out, tired.
'I've had the gong.'

goolie
A stone.
'He chucked a goolie.'

goose
An uncomplimentary term for another.
'He's a goose.'

grouse
Excellent.
'Extra grouse' is even better.

grouter
To 'come the grouter' is to act in a way which is very opportunistic or unfair.

guts
The stomach area. 'I hit him in the guts.'

gutser
To 'come a gutser' is literally to fall over or figuratively to suffer a misfortune.
'I came a gutser on that deal.'

H...

hip pocket nerve	To hit someone where it really hurts - the wallet.
holding	'How are you holding', means how much money do you have left.
hoop	A jockey.
Hughie	Euphemism for God. In the outback when it starts to rain, farmers will say 'send her down Hughie.'

jack

A multi-purpose word.
Hopefully you won't 'get the jack' (VD)
You may 'get jack of someone' (tire of them)
You may 'jack up' (refuse to do something)

jackaroo

A young male trainee farm worker. The female counterpart is 'jillaroo.'

jake

'She'll be jake' means that everything will be OK.

joker

A friendly term for a man.
'I haven't seen that old joker for years.'

jungle juice

Home made booze.

K...

king brown A large beer bottle.
From the Australian king brown snake.

king hit A big surprise punch. 'She king hit him.'

king pin A leading social or workplace figure.

knackers Testicles or family jewels.
One can also be 'knackered'
meaning very tired or worn out.

knock To 'knock' someone is to be disparaging
of them.
To 'get a knock' is to get lucky sexually.
For a woman to be 'knocked up' is to say
that's she's pregnant, 'up the duff,' or 'in
the pudding club.' For a man, the term
implies exhaustion.
To get a 'knock back' is to be refused
something - usually sexual advances.
To get a 'knockdown' to someone is to be
introduced to them.
'On the knocker' means being very much
on time.
A 'knock shop' is a brothel.

kick on To move from one party or pub to
another due to a desperate need for more
booze.

knee-trembler Sex in a standing position. Usually done
between dances at the ball.
Not recommended for the over 40's.

knockers A woman's breasts.
'She's got great knockers.'

lair
A dandy who is perceived to be showy and ostentatious. Often 'mug lair.'

larrikan
A young street rowdie or someone who is a little naughty.
'He's a bit of a larrikan.'

lash
To make an attempt.
'I'll have a lash at it.'

laughing gear
Mouth.

leg opener
Strong alcohol. Seen by opportunistic men as making women more sexually attainable.

leak

To urinate or piss.
'I'm going for a leak.'

legless

Drunk.

lob

To arrive. Usually at a party or social
event. 'What time should we lob?'

lousy

Usually means tightfisted or mean.
Can also describe someone who has body
lice.

lumbered

To be arrested.
'I got lumbered last night.'

lunatic soup

A general term for most booze.

lurk

A dubious or doubtful scheme.
'I got on to a good lurk.'

M...

map of Tasmania
A woman's pubic area. The shape of Tasmania bears a remarkable likeness to that particular part.

mate
A greeting which Aussie men give to just about anyone despite the fact that no real evidence of mateship exists. Can be friendly -'gidday mate' or threatening -'listen mate.'

matinee
Sex in the afternoon.

matress muncher Refer to backdoor bandit.

mick A Roman Catholic.

million When you're 'gone a million' you have very little hope of achieving your goal.

missus The wife, or 'she who must be obeyed.'

morning glory Many erections seem to occur in the early hours, but most proceed no further.

motser A large amount of money. 'He won a motser at the races.'

mozzie A mosquito.

mulga The bush or outback.

mungo A devotee of rugby league.

N...

nag	Racehorse.
naughty	Sexual intercourse. 'Did you get a naughty?'
nick	'Nick off!' means get lost. 'Get nicked' means much the same but is a little stronger. 'I got nicked' means that the wallopers (police) finally caught up with me.
nong	A less than bright person.
no-hoper	Don't expect much from a no-hoper be it man or horse.
nookie	A more polite word for 'naughty.'
nooner	Sex for lunch.
norks	A woman's breasts.
nosh	Food. 'Lets have a nosh up.'

O...

ocker	The uncultivated Aussie male.
on the ball	Someone who is alert and very aware of what's happening. 'He's really on the ball.'
on the blink	Something which is not working. 'The telly's on the blink.'
on the job	Male term for having sex. 'I was on the job last night.'
on the nose	Someone or something which is very smelly.
on the piss (grog)	Excessive indulgence in alcohol. 'He's on the piss again.'
on the side	Extra-marital sex. 'He's getting a bit on the side.'

paddock   A playing field.

panic merchant   Someone who is easily given to panic.

perve   To closely examine someone of the
                     opposite (or same) sex.
                     'He was perving on her.'

pig's arse!   A strong statement of disagreement.

pillow biter   A homosexual.

piss   Apart from relieving oneself, there's:
                     piss-up - a big drink.
                     piss off! - go away!
                     piss pot - a drunk.
                     pissing into the wind - a futile effort.
                     pissed off - very annoyed.
                     pissing down - raining hard.
                     piss poor/weak - a very weak effort.
                     pissed - drunk.

plonk   Wine.

pocket billiards A man covertly playing with himself.

poke   Sexual intercourse 'Did you get a poke.'

pole vault
The way a man fancies he moves around with an erection.

Pommy
What Aussies call Englishmen (affectionately)

pork sword
A penis.
Other options are:
beef bayonet
corned beef telescope
lamb lance
mutton dagger
pyjama python

posted
To be stood up.
'She left me posted.'

prang
A usually not-too-serious car crash.

prick teaser
A girl who leads a man on but has no intention of going all the way.

punt
To gamble on the horses.
Thus the term 'punter.'

put in
To 'put in the time' means to do your fair share of work.
To 'put someone in' is to inform on them.
'Who put in?' is the question asked when a quiet fart is in the air.

far

quack	The doctor. Not always uncomplimentary.
queen **queer**	Refer to back door bandit.
quickie	A very brief sexual encounter.
quid	A pound before decimal currency.
quim	Refer to map of Tasmania, hairy chequebook etc.
quoit	Bum. 'I gave him a kick up the quoit.'

race off   To take someone away for the purpose of seduction. Done overtly by males and covertly by females.

rap   To give someone a rap is to bestow generous praise.

rack off!   Means 'get lost!'

ratbag   A stupid person.

rat house   A lunatic asylum.

ratshit   Feeling crook.
'I was ratshit,' or 'I was R.S.'

rev head   A fast-driving car freak.
Also 'petrol head.'

root   Sexual intercourse.
'I got a root (Wellington boot) last night.'

rooted   Tired and exhausted.
'I'm feeling rooted.'

rubbish   To dismiss another's views.
'To rubbish someone.'

S...

schooner	A 15 oz (425 ml) glass of beer.
scoot	To depart. 'I'm going to scoot.'
scunge	A badly groomed person. 'She's a real scunge.'
shemozzle	A total state of confusion. 'It was a real shemozzle.'
shiack	To play the fool. 'He was shiacking around.'
shickered	Being shickered is not quite as serious as being pissed.
shirt lifter	A homosexual.
shit kicker	One who does manual labour or menial tasks.

shit
Has a wide variety of uses:
contempt - 'he's a real shit!'
nonsense - 'that's a lot of shit!'
defecation - 'I need a shit.'
annoyance - 'shit!'
trouble - 'in the shit.'
worthless - 'not worth a pinch of shit.'
fear - 'he scared the shit out of me.'
scarce - 'as rocking horse shit.'
mean - 'he wouldn't give you the steam off his shit.'
bad luck - 'stiff shit.'
indifference - 'he doesn't give a shit.'
bad tempered - 'shit on the liver.'
happy - 'as a pig in shit.'
good - 'he's shit hot.'

shoot through
To depart.
Leisurely - 'I think I'll shoot through now.'
Hastily - 'We'd better shoot through.'

shot
'That's the shot' means that's correct or that's good.
To 'take a shot' at something means to give one's best effort to the task.
To 'have a shot' at someone is to be critical of them.

skerrick
Usually applies to lack of food in the house.
'I haven't got a skerrick in the fridge.'

skint Broke.

slash To have a slash is to take a leak.

sling A special payment, bribe or secret commission. Winning racehorse owners often 'sling' the jockey.

sling off To deride or ridicule someone. 'She was slinging off at me.'

slug To overcharge. 'They slug you down there.'

smart arse Someone who thinks he knows everything.

smoko A work break.

snag A usually erect penis which is seeking to be planted.

snags　Sausages. 'Did you bring the snags?'

snatch　The female genitalia.

sort　A 'good sort' is an attractive woman. A 'crook sort' is the direct opposite.

sparrows fart　Early morning

squib　A coward.

squirt　Can be a drink or a piss. 'Let's go down for a squirt.' A small child - 'he's just a squirt.'

spit chips　To suffer from anger and frustration. 'The boss was spitting chips.'

stickybeak　A very inquisitive person.

stiff　To be stiff is to be very unlucky 'he was real stiff.' May also apply to a man who is about to get lucky or is dead.

stoush　A pub or street fight. 'I got into a stoush last night.'

'Straya'　Australia. Sadly, few Aussies can pronounce Australia.

sword swallower　A lady who enjoys variation in her sex life.

talent	Desirable members of both sexes. 'Let's go to the beach and check out the talent.'
tall poppie	Successful people whom the unsuccessful want to cut down to their size.
tan track	The anus.
tanked	Drunk.
tart	A man's description of a woman with a doubtful reputation.
technicolour yawn	Vomit, chunder. The contents of a chunder are usually very colourful.
tightarse	A mean and miserly person.
tin arse	Lucky. - 'He's a real tin arse.' 'He's tinny.'
tinnie	A beer can, or a small aluminium boat.

town To go to town on something is to get stuck into it - to give it your best.

traps To 'go around the traps' is to check one's regular haunts.

trot A good trot is when things are going well.

A bad trot is when things are going badly. 'He's having a bad trot lately.'

turps Alcohol, booze.
'He's on the turps.'

tweeds Men's (sometimes women's) trousers.

two bob each way To hedge your bet.
To sit on the fence.

walloper
A policeman.
Usually spoken about them rather than to them.

wedge
An extra drink that serious drinkers have if the rest of the group are a bit slow.

whinger
Someone who is always complaining.

wood
To 'have the wood on someone', is to know their weaknesses.

wombat
A sexually promiscious man. Someone who eats roots, shoots and leaves.

whizz off
To depart.'I think I'll whizz off now.'

wrap
To give something or somebody a big wrap is to lavish praise.

Y...

yack	To have a yack is to have a chat.
yakka	Work. 'That was hard yakka.'
y-fronts	Blokes' undies.
yobbo	An uncouth Aussie male.

GREAT Aussie Phrases

AS...

(Some colourful '**as**' comparisons)

angry as an ant
Ants do get quite angry when disturbed.

Australian as a meat pie
Australians are noted for their passion for meat pies.

bad as they come
A very bad person.

bald as a badger
More alliterative than descriptive.
Badgers have plenty of hair.

black as the ace of spades
Usually refers to a description of the night.
Politically incorrect today if referring to a person.

blind as a bat

bold as brass
A very forward person.

bright as a button
Refers to a very smart person.

busy as a one-armed brickie in Beirut

busy as a one-armed bill poster in a gale
Someone with a lot on his plate.

busy as a one-armed cab driver with the crabs
Try driving and scratching at the same time.

busy as a one-armed paper hanger
Equally difficult.

busy as a one-legged man in a arse kicking contest
A very difficult contest for even the able bodied.

camp as Chloe
Describes a homosexual.

camp as a row of tents
An early description of a homosexual.

cheap as chips
Something which is very inexpensive.

clean as a whistle
An efficient and effective operation.

cold as a fish
Describes lack of warmth and human emotions rather than body temperature. 'He's as cold as a fish.'

cold as a frog
Describes body temperature. 'I'm as cold as a frog.'

cold as your mother-in-law's kiss
The assumption being that mothers-in-law are less than warm blooded.

cold as a polar bear's bum
cold as a witch's tit
Presumably very cold.

cool as a cucumber
Cool as in cool, not cold.

crook as a dog
Refers to feeling unwell and is perhaps a little unfair
to our canine friends. Mostly hangover symptoms.

crook as Rookwood (Sydney cemetery)
Both rhyming and descriptive. Always refers to a hangover.

cunning as a shithouse rat
Presumably the rodent that chooses this particular
abode is more resourceful than his more conventionally
housed colleagues.

crazy as a loon
crazy as a two-bob watch
Simple minded or just plain stupid.

deaf as a post
'He's as deaf as a bloody post.'

drunk as a skunk
Obviously chosen for rhyming rather than descriptive qualities. As far as we know, skunks don't get on the piss.

dead as a dodo
A clumsy, flightless and extinct bird.

dead as a doornail
Both alliterative and descriptive.

dead as a maggot

dry as a bone
Means being very thirsty. So often used that it now is the brand name of a range of Aussie wet-weather gear.

dry as a chip
Thirsty. The potato or wood variety.

dry as a dead dingo's donger
A donger is slang for the penis.

dry as a Pommy's towel
The English were not noted for their regular bathing.

dumb as an ox
The adult castrated male of the genus.

easy as falling off a log
Very easy.

easy as shitting in bed
An unfortunate analogy.

fast as greased lightning

fat as a pig
All pigs are fat.

fit as a flea
All fleas are fit.

fit as a Mallee bull
Rough scrub country in Victoria where anything that lives has to be very fit.

fit as a trout
Trout keep fit by swimming upstream.

flat as a tack
Refers to one's wellbeing as well as topography.
'I'm feeling as flat as a tack.'

full as an all-stations train
full as a boot

full as a goog (egg)
full as a fart
full as a fat lady's socks
full as a tick
Pissed.

full as a bull's bum
Can't eat any more.

full as a fairy's phone book
Presumption being that a fairy (homosexual)
has a wide range of friends.

full as a seaside shithouse on bank holiday
Crowded.

full as a State school
State schools are often overcrowded.

funny as a fart in a phonebox

Certainly not very funny if you are in the phone box
and the fart is not yours.

game as Ned Kelly
Notorious Australian bushranger noted for his courage (or stupidity)

good as gold
A common response to the 'gidday mate, how ya goin' question.

happy as a lark

happy as Larry
Larry must be a very agreeable person.

happy as a pig in mud
Pigs enjoy wallowing in mud.

happy as a pig in shit
The same as above, but in a different medium.

happy as a possum up a gum tree
The possum is just happy to be home.

hard as nails
Very hard.

high as a kite
Pissed.

hot as hell
A very warm day.

low as a snake's belly
low as a shark's tit
Very uncomplimentary remarks about another.

lucky as a bastard on Fathers Day.
Unlucky.

mad as a cut snake
mad as a gum tree full of galahs.
mad as a hatter
mad as a meat axe
Mad insane or mad angry.

miserable as a shag on a rock
They only look miserable, they're really very happy sitting out there on a rock.

phoney as a three dollar bill
Somebody or something which is very dubious.

pissed as a fart
A curious comparison when you think about it.

pissed as a newt
Somehow this small and teetotal amphibian has become the yardstick for our level of drunkenness.

poor as a bandicoot
Of wretched character rather than being broke.

poor as a church mouse
Someone of very limited financial means.

popular as a pork chop in a synagogue
That is, very unpopular.

randy as a bull
randy as a snake
Someone with excessive sexual energy.

rare as rocking-horse shit
Very rare.

red as a beetroot

rough as bags
Someone who is considerably lacking in style.

rough as guts
Someone who is coarse or ill-mannered.

safe as a bank

safe as houses

scarce as hen's teeth
A very rare commodity.

sharp as a tack
One who is very bright and alert.

silly as a two-bob watch
Someone who is both unreliable and unpredictable.

skinny as a rake

slow as a snail

slow as a wet week in a caravan

smart as paint

smart as a whip

smooth as a baby's bum

stubborn as a mule

thick as a brick
thick as two planks
Thick as in stupid.

thin as a reed

tight as a fish's arse
Watertight. Someone who is very miserly.

toey as ten men
Someone who is anxious for action, often sexual.

ugly as a hatful of arseholes
The mind boggles at this word picture.

ugly as sin

useful as an ashtray on a motorbike
Meaning someone or something totally useless.

useful as a hip pocket on a singlet
useful as a glass door on a dunny
Useless.

useless as a bull's tit
Or a man's.

useless as a chocolate teapot
Try it one day.

useless as a handbrake on a Holden
Early Holdens were not noted for the efficiency of their handbrakes.

weak as piss
Someone lacking moral courage.
'He's as weak as piss.'

like...

(Some colourful '**like**' comparisons)

All alone like a country dunny
Outside shithouse.

All dressed up like a pox doctor's clerk
Someone dressed in cheap and gaudy clothes.

All over her like a rash
All over him like a cheap suit
Someone paying a lot of attention to another.

All over the place like a mad woman's breakfast
Confused, untidy and lacking direction.

All prick and ribs like a drover's dog
Often a description of a lean country lad.

Behaves like a moll at a christening
Wistful, pensive or confused behaviour.

Built like a brick shithouse
Applies to men or women of very sturdy build.

Carries on like a bloke with boils on his arse
Restless, agitated or just an arsehole.

Charged like the light brigade
Charged like a wounded bull
Excessive overcharging, often the restaurant bill.

Done like a dinner
Someone who is very well beaten.

Fits like a bum in a bucket
Snug.

Flat out like a lizard drinking
Extremely busy at work.

Getting on like a house on fire
Enjoying another's company.

Goes at things like a bull at a gate
Impatient and somewhat reckless behaviour.

Goes like shit off a warm shovel
Goes like a bat out of hell
Moves very quickly.

Has a face like a the back end of a bus
Has a face like the dark side of the moon
Very uncomplimentary.

Has a face like a Mallee root
Usually said by a male about a female.

Has a head like a beaten favourite
Not pretty.

Has a head like a robber's dog

Has a head like a twisted sandshoe
Very uncomplimentary remarks.

Has a mouth like a horsecollar
Large and constantly moving.

Hung like a Mallee bull
A man with above average size genitals.

In and out like a fiddler's elbow
Mostly describes a person of variable moods but can have a sexual connotation.

In like Flynn
To seize an opportunity (business/sexual)
After Australian born Hollywood actor
Errol Flynn (1909-1959)

Like a bear with a sore head
Bad tempered.

Like a bee in a bottle
Very busy.

Like a dog's breakfast
Very messy.

Like a dog on lino (linoleum)
All over the place.

Like a fish out of water
Uncomfortable and ill at ease.

Like a rat with a gold tooth

Someone who is not to be trusted - insincere.

Like a red rag to a bull

Anything which excites anger.

Like a school at Christmas

No class.

Like kissing your sister

There's not a lot in it.

Like putting Dracula in charge of the blood bank

Not recommended.

Looks like a baby's arm hanging out of a pram holding an apple

A sight often seen in mens' locker rooms.

Looks like a cocky on the biscuit tin

Smug.

Looks like a stunned mullet

Someone looking very vague and distracted.

Ran like a hairy goat

A punter's term for a slow horse.

Running around like a blue-arsed fly

Running around frantically but getting nowhere.

She bangs like a dunny door in a gale
She goes off like a bucket of prawns in the sun
She roots like a rattlesnake
Male comments about a female's sexuality which are not
always based on first hand knowledge.

Shoot through like a Bondi tram
To leave the scene quickly.

Squealed like a stuck pig

Sticks like shit to a blanket
Usually someone who won't go away.

Stood out like a bandicoot on a burnt ridge

Stood out like a cocktail bar in the Sahara

Stood out like dog's balls

Stood out like a shag on a rock
Very visible.

Up and down like a bride's nightie
Up and down like a yo yo
A person of wildly fluctuating emotions.

Up her like a rat up a drainpipe
Fast and often opportunistic sex.

Couldn't...

(expressions of **incompetence** or **indifference**)

blow the froth off a beer

fight his way out of a wet paper bag

find the grand piano in a one-roomed house

give a flying fuck

give a rat's arse

go two rounds with a revolving door

hit a bull in the bum with a handful of wheat

knock the dags off a sick canary

organise a fart in a baked bean factory

organise a fuck in a brothel with a handful of $50's

organise a piss-up in a brewery

pick a seat at the pictures

pull the skin off a rice pudding

run out of sight on a dark night

tell the time if the town hall clock fell on him

train a choko vine over a country dunny

So mean he...

still has his lunch money from school

wouldn't give a rat a railway pie

wouldn't give you a fright if he was a ghost

wouldn't give you a light for your pipe at a bushfire

wouldn't give you a shock if he owned the powerhouse

wouldn't give you a wave if he owned the ocean

wouldn't give you the steam off his shit

wouldn't give you the time of day

wouldn't give you the wind off his fart

wouldn't piss on you if you were on fire

wouldn't shout if a shark bit him

Other Aussie phrases

(A few general Aussie phrases which add colour to our language.)

a bit of all right

Usually a man speaking very favourably about a woman.

a cabbage short of a coleslaw
a chop short of a barbecue
a few bricks short of a load
a sandwich short of a picnic

Describes one who is perceived to be not too bright or not the full quid.

argue the toss

To argue against the odds or to just argue.

arse about face

A total reversal or back-to-front.
'He's got it all arse about face.'

arse beats class

When sheer good luck wins out over careful planning.

Avagoodweegend

What Aussie workmates say to each other on Friday afternoon. Also 'javagoodweegend?' which is said by the same people on Monday morning.

bag your head!

Said when your usual powers of persuasion fail you.

belt the living daylights
To give someone a good hiding.

better than a poke in the eye with a sharp stick
A poor but preferable alternative.

bite your bum!
An alternative to 'bag your head.'

bore it up 'em
A sporting term meaning to strongly press home the team's decided advantage.

break it down!
An exclamation demanding fair play.

Buckley's chance
No chance.
Sometimes stated as 'you've got your's and Buckley's.'

bun in the oven
Pregnant.

bung on a blue
To start a fight.

butter wouldn't melt in his mouth
A person of angelic appearance, but usually deceptive.

can't take a trick
A constant loser. 'I can't take a trick today.'

caught short
To have an urgent requirement to do No. 2's.

choke a darkie
To defecate.

cop a dose
To gain a very unwelcome side-effect from
getting your end in.

cop it sweet
To accept admonishment without complaint.

crack a fat
To achieve an erection.

crack hardy
To put on a brave front.

cruel someone's pitch
To spoil another's fun.
'He's doing well with that sheila but I'll try to cruel his
pitch.'

daylight second
Describes a very clear winner.

didn't come down in the last shower
Someone who is no fool and not easily led.

didn't run a drum
Usually describes a poorly-performed horse.

dining at the Y
Something that some men usually reserve for women other
than their wives. You'll have to figure it out.

do your block

To lose control of one's temper. Also 'do your nana.'

doesn't know if he's Arthur or Martha
doesn't know if he's bored or punched

Someone in a total state of confusion.

don't come the raw prawn

Don't feed me that bullshit.

draining the dragon

Urinating.

dragging the chain

Not keeping up with others in a drinking session.

drink with the flies

Someone who chooses or is forced to drink alone.

drop your bundle

To lose control of oneself. 'He dropped his bundle.'

fair crack of the whip

Be reasonable, do it my way.

fair go

A reasonable (but sometimes unreasonable) chance to achieve one's goals. Everybody wants a fair go.

fair suck of the sav

A demand for fair play.

first cab off the rank

To be the first to take advantage of an opportunity.

flog the dog (lizard)
Male masturbation.

freckle puncher
Homosexual.

gangbusters
Something 'going gangbusters' is something going very well.

gash magnet
A man who's good at pulling the chicks.

get a load
To acquire a very unwanted rash (or worse) from a bit of stray nookie.

get in for your chop
To push ahead for your share of whatever it is that's going.

getting your end in
Men come from a certain place and spend the rest of their lives trying to get back there.
Also referred to as 'getting a bit', or for a married man, 'getting a bit on the side.'

get stuck into it
To enthusiastically tackle the task at hand.
To get stuck into someone is to fight them.

getting off at Redfern
Coitus interruptus.
Redfern is just one station before Central.

give it a bash (burl)
To make an attempt.

give it the herbs
To rapidly accelerate a car.

giving the ferret a run
Sexual intercourse.
'I think I'll give the ferret a run tonight.'

go for the doctor
To go all the way. To do one's best.

go for your life
Curiously this means 'go right ahead, be my guest.'

go the knuckle
To get involved in a fist fight, or describes
someone who is very capable in this area.
'He can really go the knuckle.'

had a thirst that would cast a shadow

had a thirst you could photograph
Exaggerated but very descriptive.

half a mongrel (brute)
An oncoming erection.

had the gong
Tired, beaten, can't go on. 'I've had the gong.'

have two bob each way
To be so undecided as to hedge any bets.

hawk the fork
What ladies of the night do.

he could talk under water with a mouth full of marbles
Garrulous.

he's got death adders (mousetraps) in his pocket
Not given to buying a drink when its his turn.

he's got more arse than Jessie
(Sydney Zoo elephant)
Usually means someone who enjoys a great deal of luck but can be used to describe someone with a lot of hide (cheek)

he's got more front than Myers (retail store)
Hide, cheek, effrontery.

he's got more movements than a Swiss watch
Someone who is a bit dodgy.

he's got tickets on himself
Someone who likes himself very much.

he's in more trouble than Speed Gordon
Has big troubles.

he's missing a few spots on his dominoes
Someone a little less than bright.

he's not playing with the full deck
See 'few bricks short of a load.'

hide (sink) the sausage

Euphemism for sexual intercourse.

home and hosed

A racecourse certainty.

'He's home and hosed' or 'home and dried.'

Refers to a horse which is seen as likely to be back in the stalls while the other horses are still running.

hope your balls turn into bicycle wheels and back pedal up your arse

hope your chooks turn into emus and kick your dunny down

Great Aussie curses.

horizontal folk dancing

Sexual intercourse.

in the family way

Pregnant.

in the shit

In trouble.

It puts lead in your pencil

Certain food and drinks which are believed to increase male sexual performance.

I've had the dick
I'm finished, I can't go on.

keeping one for Ron
When offered one item,
take two and keep one for Ron (later on)

kick the tin
To contribute to a collection box or tin.

long streak of pelican shit
Describes a very tall and thin person.

living on the smell of an oily rag
Someone who manages to live on very little.

more...than you can poke a stick at
Means that you have more than ample.

munching on the muffin
See 'dining at the Y.'

my stomach thinks my throat's cut
Very hungry.

no flies on him
A very smart person.

no room to swing a cat
Very little space.

not much chop
Something inferior or very ordinary.

not the full bottle (quid)
Not super-intelligent.

not worth a cracker (sausage) (crumpet)
Worthless.

not worth a pinch of shit
Less than worthless.

on a promise
Sexual expectations. 'He's on a promise tonight.'

on the blink
Something that is not working.
'The beer's warm 'cause the bloody fridge is on the blink.'
Alternatives are 'had the dick', 'had the sword',
or just 'rooted.' 'On the blink' always applies to things,
the alternatives can also apply to people.

on the nose
Means literally, something (or somebody) which smells
badly, 'he's on the nose', or figuratively, a very suspicious
business deal.

on the outer
Someone who is not very popular.

on the white telephone
Having a chunder or technicolour yawn.
Also known as driving the big white bus.

one-eyed trouser snake
The penis or pork sword.

over the fence
Unreasonable.

park the tiger (prawn)
To get your end in.

pass in your marble
To die or cark it.

pass the buck
To place responsibility with someone else.

pay with the hairy cheque book
Sexual favours in lieu of payment.

pick the bones out of that one
A statement made by one who has just farted in company and needs to emphasise the point.

pick the eyes out of
To select the best of a number of options.

plays piano in a brothel
Someone who is actually employed but is not too fussy about how or where.

point percy at the porcelain
Yet another way for a man to excuse himself to go to that little house.

pull your head in!
Shut up!

punch the whiskers (pants)
A man's somewhat indelicate description of
getting his end in.

pushing shit up hill with a sharp stick
Someone on a hopeless mission or an enterprise
doomed to failure.

put the hard word on
To make strong sexual overtures.

put the cat among the pigeons
To create havoc.

scream blue murder
To complain loudly.

scream your tits off
For a man or a woman to make a big fuss about something.

shake hands with my wife's best friend
shake hands with the unemployed
A popular male comment made when
excusing himself to go to the Gene Tunny.

she'll be right!
Expression of reassurance.

she's seen more pricks than a second hand dartboard
A very experienced lady of the world.

shit on the liver
A presumed cause of bad temper.
'He's got shit on the liver today.'

short arms and deep pockets
Describes blokes who avoid their shout at the bar.

shut the gate
A statement made when it appears that the winner is obvious.
'He's so far in front it's shut the gate.'

sink the sausage (sav)
Euphemism for sexual intercourse.

siphon the python
Men's talk for urinating.

sling off
To ridicule someone.
'He was slinging off at me,'

slip a length
See 'getting your end in.'

so hungry...
I could eat the crutch out of a low-flying duck.
I could eat the crutch out of a rag doll.
I could eat the horse and chase the rider.

so poor...
he'll lick the paint off the fence.

spit the dummy
To throw a tantrum and stalk off in high dudgeon.

splash the boots (splash)
Male term for urination. 'I'm going for a splash.'

split the rug
Women's talk for taking a piss.

squeal like a stuck pig
To protest loudly about something.

starve the lizards!
An exclamation of frustration with another's point of view.
Not used much today.

stick it up your arse! (jumper)
A reasonably strong term of disapproval.

stone the crows!
An exclamation of annoyance or surprise.

strike a blow
To go to work.

taking the mickey / piss
Using sarcasm to put someone down.
'He took the mickey out of me.'

the elevator doesn't reach the top floor
No mental giant.

there's a light on the verandah, but nobody's home
A person who is functioning but not comprehending.

throw a leg
Men's talk for having their way.

trap for young players
A hazard for the unwary.

two palings short of a fence
Not too bright.

went mad and they shot him
'Where's Harry?' 'He went mad and they shot him.'
Usually means whereabouts unknown.

wet enough to bog a duck
Very wet.

when the shit hits the fan
You're in big trouble.

where the crows fly backwards to keep the sun out of their eyes
Describes a very remote outback place.

would kill a brown dog
Usually refers to lousy food.

wouldn't know him from a bar of soap
Someone who is very much a stranger.

wouldn't know his arse from his elbow
wouldn't know if you were up him
wouldn't know shit from clay
A vague or very dumb person.

wouldn't touch it (him) with a 40 foot pole
Something/someone who is to be carefully avoided.

wouldn't work in an iron lung
Someone who is lazy and indolent.
'He wouldn't work in a bloody iron lung!'

up a gum tree
Someone who is in trouble. Describes a situation
where there are not too many options left.

up shit creek without a paddle

Someone also facing a very difficult situation.
A more polite phrase is 'up the proverbial.'

up yours for the rent!

A strong statement of rejection.

Aussie Rhyming SLANG

Rhyming SLANG is a miscellaneous
collection of phrases based on words which lend
themselves to special treatment.

Originally made popular by the quick-witted and
waggish Cockneys in London's East End, rhyming
slang spread to other parts of the world and in particular
to Australia.

Australians with their strong English background and
taste for fun and irreverence, readily adopted rhyming
slang and made it a part of their culture.

Whilst rhyming slang tended to be used by those who
frequented pubs, clubs and racecourses, it also became
popular with a broader public particularly when a
substitute was required for a more direct and perhaps
socially unacceptable word.

Many original Cockney words are still in use in
Australia. Many were modified to suit our conditions
and others are quintessentially Australian.

Most rhyming slang words deal with everyday matters
and despite a preoccupation with drinking, gambling,
body parts and fornication, the language is essentially
good natured.

Many **rhyming slang** words are **euphemisms** - **Bengal Lancer** (cancer), **Edgar Britt** (shit), **Khyber Pass** (arse) Some imported words were used **during wars** and the **Depression** and fell into **disuse.** Others are very **recent** and are often based on high- profile **politicians, sportsmen and film and media identities.**

Australians being a very **egalitarian lot** have adopted rhyming slang across **all levels of society.**
From the outback shearing sheds this piece of Australian rhyming slang emerged.

Hey **Mark Foy** (boy), tell the **pitch and toss** (boss) that there's a **willow the weep** (sheep) in my **nine and ten** (pen) with a **civil answer** (cancer) in his **I suppose** (nose).
Shearers usually avoided shearing sheep with this nasty affliction.

Rhyming slang has its **rules.** It consists of **two or more words** the **last** of which **rhymes** with the **word** replaced. **Where applicable,** the **shedding** of the **second or rhyming word** is **encouraged.**

Example:

The rhyming slang word for road is **'frog and toad.'**
Simply drop the rhyming word **'toad'** and say **'I'm off down the frog'.**

alone	**Pat Malone** (Pat) I'm on my Pat tonight.
arms	**Warwick Farm(s)** (Warwicks) Usually refers to lack of underarm hygiene. Someone may be a 'bit woofy' (smelly) or 'Long Jetty' (sweaty) under the Warwicks. *A Sydney racecourse.*
arse (bum)	**Khyber Pass** (Khyber) Refers to the anus itself rather than effrontery (more arse than Jessie); luck (you arsey bastard); job dismissal (I got the arse); or sexual achievement (a piece of arse) For one to tell another to 'stick it up your Khyber' indicates a distinct lack of goodwill between the two. *The pass linking Afghanistan and Pakistan.* Also Tijuana Brass or Bulli Pass (Bulli)
back	**hammer and tack** (hammer) To be on someone's hammer is to pursue that person by keeping on his track or figuratively, 'back'. Also used to indicate a sudden lack of employment. 'I got the hammer' (sack)
balls (testicles)	**orchestra stalls** (orchestras) Niagara Falls town halls

bank	**J. Arthur Rank** (J. Arthur) Used literally - 'I'm going to the J. Arthur' or figuratively by punters - 'I'll put that (winnings) in the J. Arthur.' *UK film producer.*
bar	**near and far** 'I'll meet you in the near and far.'
barber	**Sydney Harbour**
bath (tub)	**Bib and Bub**
bed	**roses red** (roses) Bill and Ted Roberta Flack = sack (Roberta)
beer	**Ray Stehr** *Australian rugby league player.* Also 'Terry Dear.' *Australian radio personality.*
belly	**Ned Kelly** *Notorious Australian bushranger, (1857-1880)*
bet (to have a)	**cast a net**
bill (account)	**Jack and Jill** What you get at the end of a restaurant meal.
bog (defecate)	**hollow log** One takes a bog as opposed to leaving it.

booze	**La Perouse** (Larpa) To be, or plan to be 'on the Larpa' suggests rather more than a quiet social drink. *A Sydney suburb.*
boss	**pitch and toss** Of shearing shed origins but now used to describe authority in the workplace.
bowl (cricket)	**Nat King Cole**
bowler (cricket)	**Coca Cola**
bowlers (lawn)	**rock and rollers** A somewhat facetious but not unkind term for the mostly elderly folk who play lawn bowls.
brandy	**Fine and Dandy** *Champion Australian racehorse.*
bread	**lump of lead**

broke **hearts of oak**
Often describes lack of
success at the racetrack.

brolly (umbrella) **Aunt Molly**

bum **deaf and dumb**

butter **kerb and gutter**

cab (taxi) **Sandy McNabb** (Sandy)
left jab
smash and grab

can (beer) **Neville Wran** (Neville)
NSW premier 1976-1986.

cancer	**Bengal Lancer** civil answer Spanish dancer
cash	**sausage and mash** (sausage) Oscar Asche (Oscar) *Aussie actor (1871-1936)*
change (money)	**Kembla Grange** (Kembla) 'Keep the Kembla.' *A racetrack south of Sydney.*
cheque	**goose's neck** (goose's) Gregory Peck (Gregory) nervous wreck (nervous)
chilly	**Picadilly**
chunder (vomit)	**up and under** The chunder, or technicolour yawn, has become an Australian institution. Chunders always contain carrot fragments even when none have recently been eaten.
clock	**dickory dock**
cobber (mate)	**thief and robber**

cock (penis)   **eight day clock** (eight day)
The popular clock which lasted eight
days when fully wound somehow
contrasts with the average male
appendage. Also Rupert Murdoch.

cold   **soldiers bold (soldiers)**

cook   **babbling brook** (babbler)
Army and outback cooks not noted
for their culinary skills.

cop (policeman)   **John Hop (John)**

crap (shit)   **Andy Capp**

crook (unwell)   **butcher's hook** (butchers)
'I'm feeling a bit butchers.'
Sometimes used for 'look' as in
'Have a butchers at this.'

cunt   **Ballina Punt** (Ballina)
When one refers to another as a
'Ballina' there is obviously a serious
level of animosity between the two.
Some prefer **'All quiet on the
Western Front'** (all quiet)

curry   **Arthur Murray**
When Indian restaurants
were changing Australians'
eating habits, Arthur Murray
was teaching us to dance.

dance	**Jack Palance** US *film actor.*
daughter	**ten furlongs** = mile and a quarter
dole	**rock and roll** The curious custom of being paid for not working. 'He's on the rock and roll.'
dollar	**Oxford scholar** (Oxford) Also 'Rhodes scholar'
dope (drug)	**Bob Hope** A broad term for all illegal drugs.
double (racing)	**froth and bubble**
drink	**cuff link**
drum (racing tip)	**deaf and dumb**
drunk	**elephant's trunk** (elephants) Being 'elephants' is more socially acceptable than being drunk.
dunny	**Gene Tunny** (Gene) The classic Australian outhouse. US *heavyweight boxer.*
ears	**ginger beers**

erection	**State election**
eyes	mince pies
face	Martin Place
fart	**horse and cart** 'Who horse and carted?'
fat (erection)	**larrikin's hat** (larrikin) 'I've got half a larrikan.'
feet	plates of meat
ferry	**Chuck Berry** As seen on Sydney Harbour.
finger	Onkaparinga Engagements are formalised by placing the Frank Thring (ring) on the Onkaparinga. *South Australian blanket manufacturer.*
flowers	Cobar showers
flu (influenza)	Dan McGrew
flush (poker)	barmaid's blush
food	**Rodney Rude** (Rodney) *Australian comedian.*

fork	Duke of York
fridge (refrigerator)	Brooklyn Bridge
fuck	Donald Duck (Donald)
full (drunk)	Roy Bull 'I got a bit Roy Bull last night.'
function	Bondi Junction *Sydney's best known suburb.*
gay (homosexual)	Doris Day (Doris) Hollywood actor.
gin	Vera Lynn (Vera) *Wartime English singer.* Huckleberry Finn (Huckleberry)
gin and water	mile-and-a-quarter
girl	twist and twirl
glass (beer)	forward pass
gloves	turtle doves
Greek	bubble and squeak Werris Creek. Can be used for 'leak' - urinate.

grouse (good)

Mickey Mouse
In Aussie-speak, grouse means good
and extra grouse means very good.
Whilst grouse is rarely used today,
Mickey Mouse remains. A Mickey
Mouse result is a good result,
although it can sometimes mean
inferior quality - 'a Mickey Mouse
watch.'

guts

comic cuts (comics)
'He hit him in the comics.'

hair

Fred Astair
*American actor/dancer born
Fredrick Austerlitz (1899-1987)*

hands

German bands

harlot

apple charlotte

hat

tit for tat (titfer)

head

Kelly Ned

heart

jam tart

horn (erection)

early morn
Most erections occur in the early
morn.
Sarah Vaughan (Sarah)

horses (races)	tomato sauces
Jew	four by two (fourby) Usually spoken about Jewish people not to them.
jewellery	tom foolery (tom)
keg (beer)	Jersey Flegg *Australian rugby league player.*
kids	billy lids (billys) An affectionate term for one's own or somebody else's children.
knackers (balls)	Jatz Crackers *An Aussie biscuit.*
knees	gum trees Gypsie Rose Lee(s)
lair (a dandy)	teddy bear One, who by showy dress or ostentatious manner, achieves general contempt.
lay (sexual intercourse)	Johnny Ray *US singer.*

leak (urinate)

Werris Creek (Werris)
To 'have a Werris' is classic
Australian rhyming slang for
urinating. *A town in NSW.*

legs

bacon and eggs
fried eggs

lie

pork pie (porky)
Politicians are good at
telling porkies.

lift (car ride)

Malcolm Clift (Malcolm)
*Australian rugby league
player and coach.*

look

Captain Cook (captain)
The original Cockney for 'look' was
'butchers hook.' Now, 'have a captain
at this' is the common term.
*English explorer/navigator who
discovered Australia. (1728-1779)*

matches

Jack Scratches

mate (friend)

China plate (China)
The common form is China which
is so often abbreviated that most are
unaware that 'plate' is attached.
Used widely by Australian males
even though no real evidence of
mateship exists.

meal

Leonard Teal (Leonard)
Australian actor.

milk

Acker Bilk (Acker)
English jazz musician.

missus (wife)

cheese and kisses (cheese)
She who must be obeyed.

money

Bugs Bunny

mouth

north and south
Pronounced 'norf an souf.'

nose

I suppose
Queensland shearing shed origins
where it applied to a sheep's nose.

party

gay and hearty
'We're having a gay and
hearty next week.'

pecker (penis)

Boris Becker
A German tennis player of some note.

pee

you and me
'I'm going for a you and me.'

**perve
(lecherous look)**

optic nerve (optic)
The careful study of attractive young
ladies.
'Have an optic at that!'

**pictures
(cinema)**

flea and itches
Classic 1930's RS. People caught
the 'bread and jam' (tram) to the
flea and itches.
The term was very appropriate
to many of the picture theatres
of the time.

piddle

Nelson Riddle (Nelson)
US bandleader.
Also 'hi diddle diddle.'

pie (meat)

dog's eye

plate

Reg Date
Australian soccer player.

piss

hit and miss
This is the most popular term for this most popular subject.

angel's kiss (angel's)

Johnny Bliss (Johnny)
Australian rugby league footballer.

snake's hiss (snakes)

Shirley Bliss (Shirley)
Ex Miss Australia.

pissed

Adrian Quist (Adrian)
To some, being 'Franz', Mozart', 'Brahms', or 'Schindlers', more accurately describes the state of inebriation. Most RS. users however prefer to be 'a bit Adrian.'
Australian tennis player.

Mozart and Liszt (Mozart)
An unlikely alliance of the 18th century Austrian composer Wolfgang Amadeus Mozart and the 19th century Hungarian Franz Liszt.

Schindler's List
A Hollywood movie based on Thomas Keneally's book Schindler's Ark.

pocket

sky rocket

poof (homosexual) **horse's hoof** (horses)

poofter **willy woofter**

poor **Archie Moore** (Archie)
Describes a temporary shortage of funds rather than a permanent state of poverty. *US heavyweight boxer.*

port (wine) **Goldsborough Mort**
Early Sydney trading company.

price **curry and rice**
When asking the price of an item, Australians often use the term emmachisit?

pub (hotel) **rubbity dub** (rubbity)

pull
(masturbate) **Roy Bull**
Australian rugby league player.

punch **cut lunch**

quinella **Nelson Mandela** (Nelson)
A very recent RS word created by the horseracing fraternity.

races (horse) **airs and graces**

rain **Frankie Laine**
US singer.

razor	**Dawn Fraser** *Champion Australian swimmer.*
rent	**Duke of Kent**
ring	**Frank Thring** *Australian actor.*
river	**shake and shiver**
road	**frog and toad (frog)** To 'hit the frog' is one of the most popular of all RS phrases.
root (intercourse)	**Angus & Coote** (downtown jeweller) The getting of a 'downtown jeweller' was long a sexual boast of young Sydney men. *A Sydney jewellery firm.* Also **Ron Coote** (Ronny) *Australian rugby league player.* **Wellington boot** (Wellington)
rum	**Dad and Mum**
sack (bed)	**hammer and tack** (hammer)
sauce (tomato)	**dead horse**
set (tits)	**each way bet**
sex	**Vincents and Bex** *Old Aussie headache powders.*

schooner (beer)   **Lilly of Laguna** (Lilly)

scotch (whisky)   **Gordon & Gotch** (G & G)

scotch & water   **Gordon and ten**
Obtained from Gordon & Gotch
(scotch) and ten (furlongs) = mile
and a quarter = water.

shakes   **Joe Blakes**
Usually the aftermath of a
serious drinking session.

shark   **Noah's Ark** (Noah)

shave   **Dad and Dave**
*Popular pre-war radio serial of
the same name.*

sheep   **willow the weep**
An Aussie shearing shed term.

sheila (woman)   **Charlie Wheeler** (Charlie)
Women today prefer not to be
called sheilas or charlies.

shirt   **Ernie and Bert**

shit
: **Edgar Britt** (Edgar)
Refers to the function rather
than the end product.
One goes for an Edgar.
Famous Aussie jockey.
Also **'Jimmy Britt'** (boxer).

shits
: **tom tits**
Emotional rather than physical.
One gives another the tom tits.

shivers
: **Hawkesbury Rivers** (Hawkesburys)
A convenient rhyme despite the
fact that there is only one
Hawkesbury River.
A river north of Sydney.

shocker
: **Barry Crocker** (Barry)
Usually refers to a sportsman
having a bad game.
*Aussie actor famous for
his Bazza McKenzie role.*

shoes
: **Basin Street Blues** (Basin Streets)

short (of money)
: **Holmes a Court**
Being short of money was an
experience unknown to the late
Australian business tycoon, Robert
Holmes á Court.

shout (bar)

Wally Grout (Wally)
When its your 'Wally' its your turn
to buy the next round of drinks.
Aussie Test cricketer of the 60's.

shower

Tyrone Power (Tyrone)
Hollywood actor.

sick

Tom and Dick

silly

Uncle Willy
'Don't be Uncle Willy.'

sin

Vickers Gin

sister

skin and blister

six (cricket)	Tom Mix
skin	thick and thin
sleep	Bo Peep
smoke (cigarette)	laugh and joke
snake	Joe Blake
snooze	Tom Cruise *Hollywood actor.*
soap	Cape of Good Hope
socket (golf)	Davy Crockett *The fear of all golfers.*
socks	Joe Rocks
soup	loop-the-loop
speech	Bill Peach One may be called upon to make a Bill Peach at the next Bondi Junction (function). *Aussie TV personality.*
stairs	apples and pears
steak	off break *Cricketing term.*

story	**john dory** (JD) 'What's the JD?' Means 'what's happening?' *An Aussie coastal fish.*
suit	**bag of fruit**
sweaty	**Long Jetty** *A NSW town.*
swim	**Tiger Tim**
Sydney	**steak and kidney**
taxi	**Joe Maxi**
tea	**you and me** 'Let's have a cup of you and me.'
teeth	**Ted Heath** Barrier Reef (Barriers)
telephone	**Al Capone** This popular term immortalises the Italian-born Chicago crime boss who somehow managed to die of natural causes in 1947. Also **P**
thief	**tea leaf** Applies to those engaged in petty theft rather than serious crime.

tie	**Nazi spy**
	Dog's eye.
time	**Harry Lime**
	Of the film 'Third Man' fame.
	'What's the Harry Lime?'
tip (racing)	**egg flip**
tits	**brace and bits**
	Some prefer 'Eartha Kitts' or
	'each way bet' = set.
titties	**Bristol Cities** (Bristols)
	Original Cockney. The most popular
	term for this most popular subject.
toes	**these and those**
tool (penis)	**April fool**
toss (cricket)	**Joe Loss**
	English bandleader.
tote (totalisator)	**giddy goat** / nanny goat
towel	**Baden Powell**
	Lord Baden Powell (1857-1941)
	Founder of the Boy Scouts movement
tram	**bread and jam**

trots
(harness racing)

red hots
Early harness racing was notorious for 'arranged' race results.
'Red hot' is slang for crooked.

trousers

council houses

try (rugby)

meat pie

tub (bath)

Bib and Bub

turd

Henry the Third (Henry)
Describes the tangible result of defecation as well as being a derogatory and very unkind description of another.
King of England (1216-1272)

turner (cricket)

bunsen burner
A cricketing term for a wicket which is taking spin.

uncle

Simon and Garfunkle

undies
(underwear)

Reg Grundy's
Aussie TV identity.

waiter

hot potato
Pronounce potato as 'potatah' and the sense is maintained.

wanker

merchant banker

The term wanker was originally used to describe those who were perceived to be regularly engaged in masturbation. Now used in a broader sense to identify those whose behaviour is unusual, unpleasant or generally unacceptable.

wash lemon squash

water squatter's daughter

wave (ocean) Indian brave

whisky gay and frisky

wicket (cricket) Wilson Pickett

wide (cricket)   **Frank Hyde**
*Aussie rugby league
player and commentator.*

wife   **trouble and strife** (trouble)

wine   **Lindsay Kline**
Australian cricketer of the 60's.

winner   **baked dinner**
Punters seek a baked dinner more
than they seek a baked dinner.

wog   **Dapto Dog** (Dapto)
During WW2 'wog' was a common
and not unkind description of
those of Middle Eastern origin.
Today it seen as racist and usage
is not recommended.

worries   **River Murrays** (rivers)
Usually abbreviated to
'rivers' as in 'no rivers' or
'no wucking furries.'

Yank   **septic tank** (septic)
A somewhat unfortunate but
essentially good natured reference
to Americans.
An upmarket dunny.

See youse later!